BEE

BEES STING

From Pain

To Blessing

By Rosilin Mache Gibson

BEES STING

copyright © 2013 Rosilin Mache Gibson

All rights reserved. No part of this publication may be reproduced, stored in a retrieval system, or transmitted in any form or by any means, electronic, mechanical, recording or otherwise, without the prior written permission of the author.

BEES STING

Contents

Acknowledgements	Page vi
Foreword	Page vii
Nhamo	Page 1
Grandmother	Page 9
Jane	Page 21
Born Again	Page 31
Enlisting into the Army	Page 41
Weapons of our Warfare	Page 55
On the Run	Page 71
Agag must Die	Page 75
Afflictions of the righteous	Page 87

BEES STING

Acknowledgements:

With special thanks:

To the Holy Spirit
To All my children.

To Joyce Dayle

This book is dedicated to all who face various trials and temptations

BEES STING

Foreword

It never occurred to me that I would be editing someone else's book. Perhaps it may be possible that writers may be the best people to edit, since they sometimes have their works critiqued by non-writers. That being so, writers ought to be more compassionate to other writers. I hope that in my case this is so. My writings lacked creativity and were straight forward with the purpose to help people understand the Bible. However, in the process of editing this book, I have discovered new insights as to how to improve my own works. I have to admit that reading "BEES STING" has been an enjoyable and rewarding experience for me.

Rosilin Mache Gibson has skilfully painted pictures using words to captivate our attention. The main character, Nhamo, represents many young people who are lost and have no purpose for living. We also have his long time friend, Jane who

BEES STING

precedes him in his born again experience. Finally, the wise grandmother highlights the story and shares her experience as a Christian. She proceeds to explain that the Christian life has more to it than to just be "Born Again". There are dangers, enemies, and obstructions that lay before them that require faithfulness and spiritual maturity.

Nhamo had a past experience with the bees while trying to get the honey. These were like enemies and difficulties but his intense hunger drove him to persevere and receive the blessing. (The honey)

Maybe after reading this book I may be challenged to write a more creative book myself. May you find rich blessing and enjoy its message.

Henry Jaegers

Author, Editor and Friend

BEES STING

Nhamo

BEES STING

It was one scorching afternoon; the sun was so hot that one could literally smell it. Every living creature was hiding from the sun's rays in any place where they could find shelter from the heat. It was one of those days when even the birds found it difficult to make joyful sounds.

Nhamo was tapping the parched ground with his bare feet. The ground was very dry and hot. Nhamo was thinking about how, a few days ago, they had plenty of rain. Flowers were blooming beautifully and small creatures that feast on the flowers were rejoicing.

Nhamo passed by an overgrown swampy area and continued to cross over a small streaky stream that wound gracefully and steadily like that of a giraffe's neck. He was on his way to his grandmother's house because she was very sick. He had nothing to eat before he left the make shift home made from card board boxes because there was nothing. He sighed as he continued on his journey. Many a day he had to go without food. He thought about why it seemed that life was so unfair to him.

BEES STING

Nhamo was now very thirsty for it had been a long time since he had an opportunity to quench his thirst. Hunger was eating away at him and his stomach growled in such a way that scared him. He could not quieten his stomach. It disturbed him and caused him pain.

The sun was mercilessly beating down on him, causing little droplets of sweat to form onto his shoulder. He used the palm of his hands to remove the traces of sweat from his shoulder and licked his fingers in order to cool his tongue. Blood trickled down his leg from scratches that he received from thorns and bushes. Exhaustion, hunger and despair were taking their toll as he journeyed onward.

Nhamo cried out in agony, "Father where are you? I am languishing, disgraced and starving. I need you to help me; remember me father. When I was young, I lost my parents and I have no family and nowhere to turn to. Why don't you take me now father? I have had enough of this life? I am going to see my grandmother who is ill. I am doing a good deed

BEES STING

and is this how you repay me? Remember me father."

According to Nhamo, he received no answer. He trudged forward dragging his tired feet, and unable to lift them. Muttering to himself with his eyes blurred and unfocused, he suddenly heard the sound of bees busy collecting pollen from the flowers for their bee hive.

Nhamo stood still and listened carefully. He pinched himself to make sure that he was awake. With quickened steps, he started to make his way towards the sound. Faster and faster he walked, all fatigue was forgotten. The one thing on his mind was, "where there were bees, there had to be honey". He was right. With all of the strength that he had, he burst forward, and saw a large mahogany tree not far from him.

Little did he know that God had answered his prayer. Not far from the tree was a little stream flowing with clear water. What a miracle; as he got closer to the tree he saw a massive beehive overflowing with honey. Just the sight of

BEES STING

it made him feel full. He inched his way gingerly toward the tree.

The tree was surrounded by thorns, sharp stones and bushes. He moved slowly and carefully, getting nearer and nearer to the tree. As the stones and thorns cut his skin he felt no pain. His thoughts were only on the lovely honey. Closer he moved until he was only a few metres away. As he drew near, the sweet smell of the honey made him quicken his steps, but before him laid another problem: "The bees."

By now he was beyond caring. He boldly stepped forward and plunged his right hand into the honey comb. He pulled out his hand, covered with the honey, and started licking and eating it, chewing some live bees in the process.

He ate while the stinging of the bees continued. It never affected him; he felt nothing because his aim was to liberate himself from starvation. As his belly filled, he became thirsty and he started to feel the pain of the stings. Nhamo started walking towards the stream, looking for a particular bush his grandfather had shown him. He found it and sat down by the

BEES STING

stream. Before he sat down, he stooped beside the stream and began to lap up the water.

After filling himself with the honey, he sat down on a stone and began to rub his body where he had been stung. The good thing about this herb was that it sucked the stings out and prevented further swelling or pain; it was a natural anti-inflammatory. Now that he felt better, he was no longer anxious about surviving. The same herb also acted as a repellent. He got up and went for a second round by filling a pouch that he had with the honey for later consumption.

Finally, he was ready to continue on, knowing that he had food in his pouch. As the sun started to set, the searing heat became bearable. He walked with more vigour. He could now see swells of smoke rising into the horizon and he knew that he was close to his final destination.

He breathed a sigh of relief and he started to sing to himself, skipping along as he went on his way. For a moment he forgot the reason for his journey and the difficulty that he just passed

BEES STING

through. He began meeting folks that he knew from the village, greeting them as he went by and waving to those who were far off.

His grandmother's house stood out from the others because it was painted in a bright pink colour. By looking at her house one felt at peace. Nhamo reflected on how his grandmother had done well for herself, having built a large house with all the modern accessories. She had electricity, tapped water and a hot water tank. Nhamo was trying to recall the name of something which he had forgotten. He became excited when he heard voices coming from this box. When he first heard it years ago, he nearly jumped out of his skin (so to speak) only to be laughed at by his grandmother.

He remembered that it was called a radio. He liked listening to it because he could hear so many funny stories. He chuckled to himself as he knocked on his grandmother's door. A weak voice called him to come in.

BEES STING

BEES STING

Grandmother

BEES STING

Nhamo opened the door and let himself in. His salivary glands began to flow as the smell of fresh cooked food exuded from the kitchen area. The spotlessly cleaned room reminded him of times past when he had to get on his knees to keep the floor well-polished. It was something to be expected to find grandmother's house clean, comfortable and nice warm food. He looked at his cracked heels, dusty feet and bloody legs, feeling pathetic and out of place. He shuffled uncomfortably, being afraid of grandmother seeing him in such a condition.

Grandmother called Nhamo to enter into her bedroom. As he entered, he braced himself for a tongue lashing from her. He could see a side lamp shining by her bed side. Nhamo inched his way slowly toward her bed. There she was: her hair as white as snow. She looked very frail since the last time he saw her. It was the time when he ran away from her house after his parents died.

There was a void within that he thought he could fill by leaving. He had left five years ago with the hope of coming back as a successful

BEES STING

young man. He had dreams of success like any other young person. Unfortunately his life did not turn out that way. Everything he tried seemed to crumble and not be of any success. The emptiness within was even worse than before.

Nhamo tried his hand at some small paying jobs but was not successful. He learned how to live out in the open with the sky as his roof. He went for days without food, and had no shelter to keep him dry. As he approached grandmother's bed, he felt so ashamed, thinking that he should have looked after her all this time.

However, now that he was there, he hoped she would forgive him. He could hear her laboured breathing escaping from her weakened body, sounding like "Thomas the tank engine." Nhamo chuckled to himself, thinking that some things never change.

Welcome Nhamo, the prodigal son is back said grandmother. Prodigal son, what is she talking about? Is she going cuckoo or what Nhamo mused? Yes grandma, he answered in a

BEES STING

weak voice. Come closer son come and hold my hand, she said. Nhamo walked carefully as he tried to hide his appearance from her. He held her frail hand in his and she flinched as she reacted to roughness of them.

Grandma why did you call me the prodigal son? She replied, haven't you read the story from the Bible? No grandma, I don't have a Bible. She said I am glad I have you here son. Now go and bath, change your clothes, then come and I will tell you about the prodigal son.

Yes grandma. He seemed to have gotten away lightly, so he reasoned that she was not really feeling well

Nhamo went out of her room, and headed straight to his old room. Everything seemed the same as he had left it. He moved his hands gently over the furniture and he could still smell the furniture polish. It seemed as though someone had kept the room nice and clean for him.

He turned around, grabbed his towel, and headed for the door. Rules had to be followed.

BEES STING

One does not keep grandma waiting. He ran the bath and dropped some salt in the water in order to sooth his aching body. The water was nice and warm and Nhamo did not remember the last time he had a nice long soak in the bath.

As he lay in the bath he reflected on the events that had transpired in his life. As he reflected, he realised that there was something missing no matter how much he tried to deny it. What is it? He began to question himself but was no wiser. Maybe grandma knew. He promised himself that he was going to find out from her. Somehow she always seems to have answers to everything.

Nhamo was really surprised that he did not receive a tongue lashing from grandma. He felt sorry for her in her being so weak.

He finished bathing, oiling himself and dressed in clean clothes. Nhamo made his way to grandma's room where he found her propped up in her bed. She nodded as she acknowledged his presence. She invited him to sit by her side; he pulled a chair next to her bed.

BEES STING

Pass me my Bible grandma said. He passed the Bible to her ,

She had him turn to this passage:

"And he said a certain man had two sons: and the younger of them said to his father, Father, give me the portion of goods that falleth to me. And he divided unto them his living.

And not many days after the younger son gathered all together, and took his journey into a far country, and there wasted his substance with riotous living.

And when he had spent all, there arose a mighty famine in that land; and he began to be in want.

And he went and joined himself to a citizen of that country; and he sent him into his fields to feed swine.

And he would fain have filled his belly with the husks that the swine did eat: and no man gave unto him. (*He was forced to eat the swine's swill. In Satan 's kingdom nothing is for free ,the devil will always come back for what*

BEES STING

he thinks is his. It does not matter how long it takes or how high the price.)

And when he came to himself, he said, How many hired servants of my fathers have bread enough and to spare, and I perish with hunger!

I will arise and go to my father, and will say unto him, Father; I have sinned against heaven, and before thee, And am no more worthy to be called thy son: make me as one of thy hired servants.

And he arose, and came to his father. But when he was yet a great way off, his father saw him, and had compassion, and ran, and fell on his neck, and kissed him. And the son said unto him, Father, I have sinned against heaven, and in thy sight, and am no more worthy to be called thy son. But the father said to his servants, Bring forth the best robe, and put it on him; and put a ring on his hand, and shoes on his feet:

And bring hither the fatted calf, and kill it; and let us eat, and be merry: For this my son was dead, and is alive again; he was

BEES STING

lost, and is found. And they began to be merry. Make merry, and be glad: for this thy brother was dead, and is alive again; and was lost, and is found.
(Luke 15:11 – 32)

As he finished reading grandma asked him if he understood the story. She went on to explain that just as the father welcomed his son that is how she felt when he had entered the room. Grandma went on to say that in the same way your heavenly father rejoices when you come back to Him.

Grandma, who is this heavenly father Nhamo asked? (His parents never told him about Him) You never said anything in the past about Him. Why Now? Why are you doing this? Nhamo said he didn't want to be sent to any stranger called "Heavenly Father" How can Heaven have a Father? Nhamo didn't understand and thought that grandmother needed to rest. He thought that she was tired and her brain seemed to be playing tricks on her.

Grandma sighed and looked down on the quilt that covered her legs. Nhamo remembered

BEES STING

that grandma was given that quilt on her 80th birthday 5 years ago by his mother. She adored it and used it so much that he wondered what would happen if it was torn or stolen. Anyhow chances of it being stolen were zero since the person would have to steal grandma too. Now Nhamo watched her stroking it lovingly as if it had bones that could break.

She lifted up her face with an expression that he never expected. Then she said son listen to me. You can go about searching for things you don't even know or understand, but you will never find them. The prodigal son went searching for something he never found. That applies to you, you left this place in search of something and returned empty and now you are back.

Nhamo gazed towards the window and he could see the hens and the chicks being rounded and put into the chicken run. It was evening time and he thought of his grandma's words and was afraid to admit to himself that she was right, that deep inside he still felt empty. Could it be that she knew what was missing and what

BEES STING

he needed? Maybe she could help him find the missing link.

The thoughts were comforting as he turned around and looked at her. He said, grandma you are still the same. You are so full of wisdom and I hope you will help me find some meaning and purpose for my life. He told her. She bid him goodnight since the excitement had left her too exhausted. It had been a long day and she was tired and he likewise was ready to go to bed.

He bade her good night and left her room. As he was leaving she called to him to bring her a glass of water. Nhamo got her some water kissed her on her wrinkly cheek and left her room.

Nhamo went to the dining room and there was no one there. He wandered into all the rooms but found no-one. He realised that the maid who cooked and gave personal care to his grandmother had finished work for the night and had left. So it was he and grandma who were left alone in that large house.

BEES STING

Nhamo started to think that his grandmother thought that he was there to look after her. If so, she was kidding herself. He was only there until she started feeling better then he would leave. He intended to leave before she told him about her Heavenly Father and how he reminded her of the prodigal son.

But that was a very interesting story thought Nhamo. If he was the prodigal son's father he would have kicked him out and told him to leave without even entertaining whatever rubbish he had for an explanation. That father must really have been desperate for a son.

Enough of this sighed Nhamo as he lowered himself onto his bed. He had forgotten how the bees stung him. Ooh that was awful. One day he would tell his children about it. Which story would he really tell them; the stinging of the bees or the sweetness of the honey, time will tell.

BEES STING

BEES STING

Jane

BEES STING

Early in the morning the sound of dogs barking, the cock crowing and the birds making a joyful sound woke him up. Nhamo had a lovely nights sleep and he was ready to face the day. He gave himself time to adjust to the surroundings and to clear his head.

Life was one long winding road slowly inching its way to its final destination, no-one knowing where. If his parents could speak they would tell him about it. Nhamo really missed them but he had to go on living. He wondered if there was any life beyond the grave. This reminded him of when he was eating the honey and was chewing on some bees in his haste. Maybe the afterlife of those bees was in his stomach, being processed and later being disposed.

He thought about, when a person is buried, their body is eaten by the worms that digest the flesh in their bellies then disposes the by-products which turn into manure. King Solomon, considered one of the wisest men on earth at according to the Bible, pondered these questions as well. Consider these words:

BEES STING

"All go unto one place; all are of the dust, and all turn to dust again. Who knows the spirit of man that goes upward and the spirit of the beast that goes downward to the earth."

(Ecclesiastes 3:20,21)

King Solomon recognized the difference between the end of man and the end of the beast, that they were not the same.

Nhamo imagined going down the road and scooping some manure from the forest. They could be his parents' remains. What a chilling feeling it gave. Nhamo decided to get up before grandma.

Nhamo got up and carried out all of his personal care. He made his bed and put away everything leaving his room nice and tidy. He opened the window and took a deep breathe of the fresh air; hungrily his lungs sucked in the clean fresh air. He wondered who ever took the time to create the trees, air, birds, grass,

BEES STING

animals you name it. Whoever did is beyond human intelligence, he thought.

Look at that lizard just lounging behind those leaves, ready to snatch an unsuspecting fly. Everything has its purpose whether small or great, thin or fat, short or tall. It is amazing. Nhamo wanted to know that person and ask him some of his questions.

He left the window and stealthily walked past all the rooms to his grandmother's room. He knocked on her door and the maid who cared for her came to answer the door. They greeted each other and she told Nhamo that she was getting his grandmother ready and he should give her half an hour. He left and went outside and walked around the yard.

Everything seemed to be celebrating and bowing to some invisible master. He felt alone because he had no-one. He looked at the third house from his grandmother's and he remembered his first girlfriend Jane. He used to like her very much. He remembered that his feelings for her were deep. He wondered what happened to her, maybe she found someone

BEES STING

else. Maybe they would meet again. He watched Mr Gore shuffle past Jane's house looking very old, leaning on his stick as he went by.

He turned and went back inside. He went into the lounge and sat down with a book in his hand. Unfortunately he could not concentrate. He put the book down and started to think about his life. He had left this house five years ago with a little bag full of his belongings. He wanted to go and find something more than what he presently had. There had to be something better, he thought. He believed that he would be able to recognize it if it dropped in front of him. He just knew that when he saw it he would know.

After first leaving his grandmother's house he went to a friend who lived in the city. When he got there he could not get a job, all his clothes were worn out and he was left with nothing. His friend kicked him out of his house. For days and months Nhamo slept on the street, with nothing to shelter him from Mother Nature. Then he met one of the elders from the village

BEES STING

who told him that his grandmother was ill, and he had to go to her.

When Nhamo heard this he knew that caring for his grandmother was the right thing to do. His trip was difficult as his shoes were worn and made walking painful. He kept walking until he had gone far enough to the point where he could not turn back.

As he entered his grandmother's house he noticed some movement coming from her room. Because the door was opened, he proceeded to go and talk to her. To his surprise the maid, who cared for her, came leading his grandmother out of her room. Grandmother looked different from the way that he saw her previously.

Grandma you look different today. What happened to you? Nhamo asked. "The Master visited me and touched me." I am starving can I please have some breakfast asked grandma, as though she had not heard Nhamo 's question. She continued her statement "His mercy rewrote my life. I should have had my soul cast down to eternal damnation, but His mercy rewrote my life.

BEES STING

There is therefore now no condemnation to them which are in Christ Jesus, who walk not after the flesh, but after the Spirit." (Rom 8:1)

Despite all that I have done in the past God has forgiven me and I am free. The Master my Heavenly Father, my Redeemer rewrote my life and the course of my life was changed. I give Him glory. Had it not been the Lord on my side where would I have been?" Grandmother had her arms lifted in the air as she made these declarations. Nhamo just gazed at her in silence.

We sat down to a lovely breakfast talking about the good old days. We laughed and reminded each other of the past. As we finished there was a loud knock on the door. The maid opened the door and led the visitor into the lounge where grandma and Nhamo were seated. Nhamo's heart skipped a beat as he raised his eyes to look at the visitor. Their eyes locked up and Nhamo's feet felt too weak to support him, he could not stand up.

BEES STING

She called his name in greeting and he answered in a weak response. Jane went to my grandma and greeted her joyfully and sat next to her. Nhamo regained his composure and joined in the conversation with Jane and his grandmother. They chatted for a while, catching up on all the village's events.

All of a sudden Jane looked at grandmother and said: I came to tell you something very important. I listened to you when you spoke to me a few months ago about our Heavenly Father. I finally met Him said Jane. Grandmother made a whooping sound and her eyes lit up with joy. Nhamo wondered what they were talking about.

So you have met this Heavenly Father. What does He look like? What does He do? Does He live close by? Asked Nhamo. Jane turned to grandma in surprise and asked her why she had not told him. Grandmother said she did not have an opportunity but now was the right time to introduce Nhamo to Our Heavenly Father.

Jane turned to Nhamo and said you see Nhamo I am now born again. What? Nhamo

BEES STING

asked in shock, surely there is something in this village that is making people go crazy. It could be the water they are drinking, he thought. Did you go back into your mother's womb, so you could be born again? Jane giggled and looked at Nhamo with the gentle eyes, and started to explain to Nhamo that Born Again is a term Jesus used to describe the need for people to experience a new purpose in life. A man named Nichodemus asked the same question to Jesus that you just asked.

"Nicodemus saith unto him, how can a man be born when he is old? Can he enter the second time into his mother's womb, and be born? Jesus answered, Verily, verily; I say unto thee, except a man is born of water and of the Spirit, he cannot enter into the kingdom of God.

(John 3; 3,4)

As Jane continued to speak, Nhamo and grandmother became much focused. Grandma spoke and said, Jane why don't you share with us how you became born again? How

BEES STING

did it all begin and what changes has God made in your life?

BEES STING

Born Again

BEES STING

I have been looking forward to sharing my experience with others. It began one day while I was talking to grandma. I shared with her the searching and the emptiness that there was in my life and although I was basically a good person there was still something missing. Nhamo thought to himself, this is starting to get interesting. How did she know what I was going through?

I started by reading the Bible for the first time and of course I started at the beginning. I was fascinated by the way the Bible described how God created everything. It seemed as though I was not just reading another book. I sensed the presence of God as I began reading its pages. I saw how things happened just by God speaking to them and I realize he was the God of great power. I noticed also how everything was created in an orderly way and I saw God as being an intelligent God. Then as I continued reading I saw how God created man and why he created him and I discovered something about God's love for him. He created man giving him freedom of choice and responsibility to exercise that freedom. He was

BEES STING

created in the image of God. That means just like God he was perfect and the choices he made were perfect.

But giving man the freedom to choose is not complete. God placed one restriction on Adam. He said everything in the garden is yours to have freely however this one tree in the middle of the garden that is off-limits. It is the tree of the knowledge of good and evil. You see God did not want man to know evil. He wanted man to continue making the right choices. To help him stay away from the tree and not make the wrong choice he created a woman to help him. But things don't always work out the way they're supposed to.

One day in the garden Adam and his wife came across a strange creature. The Bible calls him the serpent and that he is crafty. By crafty, it means he knows how to deceive and cause people to believe his lies. He spoke to Eve telling her things about God to make doubt what God had said. He made her think that God was evil and he didn't have their best interests in mind. The serpent had a name. His name was Satan

BEES STING

and he was an enemy of God. Satan was once God's angel:

> *"How art though fallen from heaven, O Lucifer, son of the morning how art thou cut down to the ground , which didst weaken the nations!*
>
> *For thou hast said in thine heart I will ascend into heaven .I will exalt my throne above the stars of God: I will sit upon the mount of the congregation, in the sides of the North: I will ascend above the heights of clouds: I will belike the Most High."(Isaiah 14:12-14)*

Eve listened to him as he told her that eating the fruit from the tree would make them like God (they were already like God*)" So God created man in His own image, in the image of God created he him: both male and female created He them" Genesis 1:27* but

he told them that God was holding something back and didn't want them to know what He knew. Eve's curiosity got the best of her and she ate the fruit and gave some to her husband who

BEES STING

was with her, and found out immediately that God was right. They would surely die. They didn't know exactly what dying meant but something strange happened that caused them to feel separated from God. That's what death is; being separated from God.

All of a sudden fear and guilt filled their minds and they found it necessary to hide. That's what sin does to us. That was bad news the day that Adam and his wife disobeyed God. Although they hid themselves, God in His great love came looking for them. He called for them, found them and asked what they had done. God knew what they did and God knew what was happening. As they stood before God clothed and their fig leaves they made excuses and blamed each other for their problem and finally wound up blaming Satan. But lying and making excuses will never cover our sin. As I thought about it I saw myself in Adam and Eve said Jane. I think of the many times I tried to excuse the wrong things that I did and blame others rather than taking responsibility for myself. The fig leaf covering of Adam and Eve are the same

BEES STING

as the excuses and the blame we use to keep us from making things right.

This story has a beautiful ending. Eventually Adam did confess and God provided a different covering for their sin. God made coats of skins and clothed them. The lesson I learned from this is that only God can take away my sin and my guilt and when I confess to him my wrong he covers me with his covering said Jane. God is a holy God and sin cannot stay in his presence. We cannot come into God's presence without His first making a way for us. With Adam it was coats of skins but for us it is his perfect son the Lord Jesus Christ.

Later on the history we find another Adam sent by God. He is called the second Adam but He was perfect just like Adam was and had a choice like Adam had but instead of choosing evil he chose only to obey God. He was tempted like Adam but never yielded to that temptation. Jesus was God's plan for the ages for man to find complete forgiveness from God. Jesus the perfect man died for me the corrupt sinner in order to satisfy the holiness of God and become

BEES STING

a perfect sacrifice. Instead of me having to die for my own sin God has allowed Jesus to take my place. I am forgiven, and set free to serve the one who took my place Jane shed a tear as she continued.

Before Jesus came into my life I was like a prisoner with the death sentence over my head condemned to die. But Jesus came, paid my bail (so to speak), and I am set free. No longer do I choose to go back to that prison house of sin but rather my goal is to live for Him who made that freedom possible. Realizing that I have been forgiven and all of my past sins are forgiven and removed I am now clean and given a new chance for freedom. That's what born again really means. Cleansed pardoned and set free. Not freedom to serve myself but freedom to serve the master who saved me, she reached out into her hand bag and brought out a tissue paper to wipe away the tears that were now freely flowing from her eyes.

Grandma encouraged me to read many places in the Bible but the one that has made the greatest impact on me was the verse found

BEES STING

in Revelation chapter 3:20. As I read this verse I knew I was in the very presence of God and His first word to me was "behold". Before that the words "I know thy works" rang clearly in my mind and I imagined that what God saw was the sin and neglect of my past life. And now he was saying behold, listen, I am here, pay close attention. "I stand at the door and knock;" can you hear me? I am knocking I had knocked before I have knocked often and now I am knocking again can you hear me?

There's a door and the handle is on the inside where you are. Will you open that door? "If any man hear my voice and will open the door I will come in." That is a promise that God will keep. The choice is mine I merely have to invite Him to come in. And the promise he gives us "and I will come in to him and sup with him and he with me". That's just like it was before Adam fell. He had communion with God all the time and now God is calling us back to that place of complete fellowship. We are reconciled in other words we are made one with Him again. He has made it possible for me to become his child.

BEES STING

As I thought of these words, wonder filled my heart, I was overwhelmed by the love of God for me and I felt so helpless and cried out to him, "Lord have mercy on me I am a sinner". Things are not the same anymore since Jesus has become my Lord and Saviour. My life is full of gratitude as I think about his great love for me and what he has done Jane was now sobbing uncontrollably.

As Nhamo heard Jane's testimony he sensed God doing the same work in himself . He began to understand and he cried out, Grandma what do I need to do, he asked. She replied, repeat after me the following and believe, then you too shall be saved.

Let us pray

Heavenly Father we thank you for who you are. We believe that you are the creator of Heaven and Earth. Lord we have sinned against you and today we ask you to forgive us in the name of your only begotten son Jesus Christ. We confess that Jesus Christ is the son of God. That He was crucified, He died and He was buried. But

BEES STING

on the third day He rose again and now He is seated on the right hand side of our Father. And we believe that He is the true son of God.

We thank you for accepting us as your children in Jesus name we pray Amen

If you have prayed that prayer well come to the Kingdom of God. You are now the sons and daughters of God. You are now the prodigal son who has come back to your father. Angels are rejoicing in Heaven. But hold your breath, because this is only the beginning of your journey.

WELCOME

BEES STING

Enlisting into the army

BEES STING

Grandma seemed to be growing stronger and stronger every day. This morning Nhamo woke up to the sound of her voice singing

> **Jehovah is your name,**
>
> **Mighty warrior great in battle**
>
> **Jehovah is your name.**

He felt very happy in his heart and he wondered what had happened. Then he remembered that he had a new life. If Jesus can change my situation to pass from death to life surely I will give Him everything I have thought Nhamo. There is nothing you can give to Jesus except your sins because all other things belong to Him.

Nhamo got up and went to the kitchen to make himself a cup of tea. Just as he was enjoying his cup of tea he heard a knock on the door. He opened the door and Jane was standing outside. Nhamo welcomed her and offered her a cup of tea. She accepted it and they sat down together and had a nice comfortable chat.

BEES STING

She told him that since she became a Christian, she faced many challenges that caused her to wonder if she did the right thing by accepting Jesus Christ. Nhamo wondered why that was so since he thought that everything would change and in a few months he would be driving a fast and most beautiful car than he could ever imagine.

Nhamo said, last night he went to bed imagining that everything would begin to move smoothly. Now you are telling me something contrary to what I was thinking, Nhamo retorted. I also am confused said Jane, that is why I came early in order for grandmother to answer some of my questions.

At that moment they heard a cough behind them and there grandma stood unexpectedly before them. They both called good morning to her at the same time. She bade them good morning and she looked so happy and fresh. If anyone walked in and they told them that she had been ill, no one would have believed them.

Grandma sat in her favourite chair by the window and asked for a glass of milk. Nhamo

BEES STING

stood up quickly and brought some to her. Jane did not waste any time asking grandma her questions. She asked grandma why everything seemed to be going wrong since she became a Christian. Grandma chuckled and shifted a bit in her chair, making herself comfortable.

She gazed at us with her loving eyes and cleared her throat in order to speak more clearly. We waited expectantly for her to enlighten us. Children, when you become born again you are like a soldier who has enlisted in the army. The army we are talking about is not a physical army where you see soldiers matching up and down. It is a spiritual army. When you come to Christ you become the devil's enemy number one. His aim is to discourage you so that you will return back to him. It does not mean that when you become a Christian things will be nice and smooth. Remember we are still living in a fallen world. That began when Adam and Eve sinned.

"***For we know that the whole creation groaneth and travaileth in pain together until now.***"

BEES STING

(Romans 8:22)

We expect to have everything nice and smooth after Jesus Christ comes back.

"For we know that if our earthly house of this tabernacle were dissolved, we have a building of God an house not made of with hands ,eternal in heavens.

(Corinthians 5:1-2)

"For in this we groan, earnestly desiring to be clothed upon with our house which is from heaven."

(2 Corinthians 5:2)

Jane turned around and said, grandma, sometimes I feel that I am all alone in this battle. Everything I try to do seems to be going the opposite way than I expected. I am beginning to lose hope. Do not be discouraged said grandma, I Will show you what others went through before you and what others are still going through even now. Let me explain what it means to be in the army of God.

BEES STING

*"**F**or we wrestle not against flesh and blood, but against principalities, against powers, against the rulers of the darkness of this world, against spiritual wickedness in high places."*

(Ephesians6:12)

Our enemies are not human, but Satan constantly uses human beings to carry out his wicked schemes. **Principalities** are rulers or beings of the highest rank and order in Satan's kingdom. **Powers** rank just below the principalities. **Rulers of darkness** are those who carry out the instructions of the powers. These represent fallen angels who are a part of Satan's army. These can never possess a human body, however, **the spiritual wickedness** are demon spirits which can actually possess a persons body.

Each evil spirit has its function and does not move from it. They work in ranks like a military army and each has his assigned task. Each functions on a different level. For example, a baby Christian will be tormented by a lesser

BEES STING

spirit than that of a mature Christian (so to speak).

In Psalm 91:3, the snare of the fowler, and from the noisome pestilence

These are demon forces of darkness that oppose Christ. They operate in large numbers , that is why they are called noisesome pestilence. (Which means a rushing calamity; one that sweeps everything before it. similar to a great Tsunami.) When these demons attack they come in a swarm like the bees , therefore, a person finds himself confronted with attacks from all ankles. Imagine a swarm of bees attacking you. Nhamo remembered the bees which attacked him a few days ago. As he thought about this, it really struck him. He thought, If demons attack in this fashion then I have to really be strong.

Grandma, is that why when things were going well for me, suddenly I lost my job, and my house that I was secure in, my house was repossessed, the boy who was going to marry me jilted me and I had creditors calling me from everywhere? The list is endless and I started to feel very overwhelmed. That is right

BEES STING

Jane, said grandmother, that's how they operate.

The terror by night; nor for the arrow that flieth by day; nor for the pestilence that walketh in darkness; nor for the destruction that wasteth at noonday.

(Psalm 91:5)

Here we have the **terror by night** which speaks of the spiritual darkness of Satan. The **arrow that flies by day** refers to the deliberate effort by Satan to destroy the soul. He does this through tempting, oppressing or trapping the believer and then shoots it as like an arrow. The arrow is normally shot so precise that it does not miss.

*"**Nor for the pestilence that walketh in darkness; nor for the destruction that wasteth at noonday**."*

(Psalm91:6)

The pestilence that walks in the darkness pertains to every scourge of satanic darkness. **The destruction that wastes at**

BEES STING

noon day refers to Satan's destroying great multitudes. Much is being destroyed by these powers of darkness.

Nhamo looked at his grandma with quizzing eyes, and asked what to do when all these powers are unleashed on him? Grandma said that it was a good question. She then told him to open

(*Colossians 2:15*)
"And having spoiled principalities and powers, he made a shew of them openly, triumphing over them in it."

Who did that, Nhamo asked in surprise? Grandma looked at him and said Jesus Christ whom you confessed to yesterday. How did He do that grandma? He went to the cross where He was crucified, He died and was buried. On the third day He rose again defeating the devil and all his hosts. When Jesus died, Satan could do no more to Him. When Jesus arose from the dead the tables turned on Satan. He was now the defeated one and Jesus was like a conquering warrior and would now be forever undefeatable. He now stands with us helping us to win our battles.

BEES STING

The devil and his henchman had a hold over us because of sin. It was like we were in prison. When Jesus died, His death was the accepted payment by God for our sins. God has declared us to be pardoned and cleansed. Because of this, Satan's claim upon us is no more. Jesus is now the captain of our salvation and we are free from Satan. We are now Children of the Heavenly Father. That does not mean that Satan cannot tempt us (he did Jesus) It means that with Jesus abiding within, we can now say No to temptation because Jesus is our helper. That is where prayer is necessary. When we are tempted, we pray and God helps.

At Calvary the blood was shed, At the resurrection the triumph is complete and Satan's captivity of us was destroyed. To understand what Born Again means, it is like being let out of prison and we are set free to serve the one who saved us. We now live in faith and thanks giving whereas under Satan we lived in constant fear. The word repentance means that because Of Jesus setting me free, I am determined to never go back to that old life again.

So grandma, you are saying that we are soldiers going to war with victory already on our side. That is right, replied grandma. We already

BEES STING

have the victory on our side. It does not matter how many times the devil and his henchman attack us. Because of Jesus our Saviour, we are more than conquerors

"Nay, in all these things we are more than conquerors through him that loved us. For I am persuaded, that neither death, nor life, nor angels, nor principalities, nor powers, nor things present, nor things to come, 39 Nor height, nor depth, nor any other creature, shall be able to separate us from the love of God, which is in Christ Jesus our Lord."
(Romans 8:37)

So you see no matter what the difficulty is that you are going through, victory is yours. When I think of the Cross, I see the arms of Jesus and I hear him saying, ***"O Jerusalem, Jerusalem, you who kill the prophets and stone those sent to you, how often I have longed to gather your children together, as a hen gathers her chicks under her wings."*** This reminds me of a story I heard from a friend which is this:

One cold night years ago in North Carolina I went outside to check on some animals housed

BEES STING

in her father's small barn. There was a full moon shining down brightly above the pines. It was so cold that the water in the horses' trough had frozen, unusual for that coastal region.

As she went to get an axe to chop through the ice, she noticed a yard hen chicken, perched near the trough, with several birdies tucked under her wings. She was impressed with how she had turned her face and frail body of fluff into the icy wind. Her wings were outstretched and it seemed to her, that she was tied, in the process of taking care of her children. My friend was uplifted by what she took to be a gift and encouragement to her faith, showing by this visual how Jesus cares for us all tirelessly.

But it struck her that those chicks had come to the hen. My friend didn't know if she chased them around the yard first in order to gather them. Some came more willingly than others, and maybe others were still out there half – frozen. (There were a few late arrivals perched on top of her wings.) She only observed that the chicks she could see, had allowed themselves to be gathered up and protected. They had quit fighting what they had no control over and finally said, "You do it, Mom."

BEES STING

And there is Jesus, dying a slow and terrible death, with his arms pulled wide. The cross is God's passionate invitation to us to come in from the cold. You are invited to the cross, it is free and everyone who will come to the cross will be saved.

"What shall we then say to these things? If God be for us, who can be against us?
(Romans 8:31)

"The LORD is my light and my salvation; whom shall I fear? The LORD is the strength of my life; of whom shall I be afraid? When the wicked, even mine enemies and my foes, came upon me to eat up my flesh, they stumbled and fell. Though an host should encamp against me, my heart shall not fear: though war should rise against me, in this will I be confiden"t.
Confess these spiritual tools day in and day out loudly.

(Psalm 27:1-2)

BEES STING

Its time for me to go for my walk grandma said as she stood up, and straightened her clothes then she left. Jane and I knew that our discussion was closed for the time being. Jane left because she had some errands to run. I left to catch up with some old friends.

Let us Pray

Adonai I come to you today and I ask you to give me strength that I may be able to stand. In times of hardship I put all my trust in you. Make me a true soldier of the gospel in executing, defending and practising your word, according to 2 Timothy 2:3 Thou therefore endure hardness, as a good soldier of Jesus Christ. No man that warreth entangled himself with the affairs of *this* life; that he may please him who hath chosen him to be a soldier. Empower me Lord that I will be able to fulfil that you chose me for. I pray that you unite us as the body of Christ that we may fight a good fight. Teach us to be obedient to your word Father. I pray this in Jesus name.

BEES STING

Weapons of our warfare

BEES STING

Nhamo woke up to the singing of the birds. In the distance he could hear the chattering of the monkeys. He wondered what their conversations were all about. He supposed that like some of us they were chatting about the day to day battles that they faced. He arose and stood by the window to let in the sweet morning breeze.

Nhamo looked up at the sky, It looked as blue as forget- me- not flowers. Far in the east he could see streaks of silver clouds forming. Maybe sometime today it might rain, he thought. A nice breeze was blowing, causing the grass surrounding their house to echo a soft melodious sound calling for the rest of the creation to join in.

God never stops amazing me, he thought. He is awesome. Who would ever think of all this? He needed to get going, tidy up his room, shower and then join grandma and Jane to find out how much he needed to pay for weapons for this warfare.

Anyone going to a Battle has to be prepared and Nhamo was going to make sure

BEES STING

that he had everything that he needed for the battle. He just hoped that they were not too expensive and within his means to purchase. Soon he would find out if he needed a uniform. He reasoned that no soldier goes to war without a uniform. He hoped the uniform would look good on him and He wondered if Jane already had hers.

After getting ready, he made his way outside for his morning walk. He followed the meandering path until he got to the end where it branched to the left. In front of him was a field full of wheat. It was wheat as far as the eye could see. Everything looked perfect. He spent some time gazing at the vast expanse of the golden grain awaiting the harvest.

As he made his way to grandmother's house, he spoke to people that he met along the way. By now the sun was starting to get hot. He loved it when he could walk on his bare feet without a care in the world as to how he appeared to others. He saw Jane in the distance heading towards his grandma's house and he

BEES STING

quickened his steps because he did not want to miss anything.

He got there just as she was getting seated. He cheerfully greeted her and his grandma who was showing off her knitting to Jane. What a wonderful thing to commune with one another with love and respect. He went to get Grandma's Bible and a cup of tea for both of them.

Grandma, settled with her Bible and tea, began to share. Children, she said, we have a busy day today because we are going to talk about some serious issues. Grandma, Nhamo spoke, since I am a soldier of Christ I want to know about the weapons I will need to fight. Are you going to measure my uniform today asked Nhamo innocently? Grandma laughed so hard that he thought she was going to pass out. He started to wonder what he had said to cause her to behave like that. He turned to Jane who was also in a fit of laughter. Not realizing the humour of the moment he merely shrugged his shoulders and muttered to himself that one can never understand women.

BEES STING

When they stopped laughing and grandma finished wiping the tears from her eyes, she looked at him and patted the chair next to her for him to sit in. He sat down still confused and not sure of what the joke was, if there was any at all. He sat down and watched Jane take her seat opposite him. Grandma sipped her tea and arranged herself in the chair and coughed to clear her throat.

Always remember that our weapons are not carnal like the guns, bombs or anything that is used to physically kill people.

"*For the weapons of our warfare are not carnal but mighty in God for pulling down strongholds, casting down arguments and every high thing that exalts itself against the knowledge of God, bringing every thought into captivity to the obedience of Christ."*
(2 Corinthians 10:4-5.)

Our God is a God of love and does not commission us to kill in His name. He does not require blood sacrifice from any human being who is full of sin. Do not let anyone mislead you into believing that by killing others you are doing God a favour. God does not need our favour. We

BEES STING

are the ones who need favour from Him and that can only come through receiving Jesus Christ as our Lord and saviour. Don't let anyone deceive you into believing that if you strap a bomb to yourself that you will get to heaven with seven virgins waiting for you. That is another one of Satan's lies. The only marriage that will take place in Heaven is the one between Christ and His church. Those who teach such lies will not be part of that wedding.

Nhamo and Jane fell into a fit of laughter when they thought about this. Grandma, you have such an imagination. Who would do that? It's true and it has been taught to others by religious people to encourage their followers to engage in violence, that is why God says:

"My people are destroyed for lack of knowledge: because thou hast rejected knowledge, I will also reject thee, that thou shalt be no priest to me: seeing thou hast forgotten the law of thy God, I will also forget thy children. As they were increased, so they sinned against me: therefore will I change their glory into shame."
(Hosea 3; 6 ,7)

BEES STING

Now let us start with the uniform that you need. Just like any soldier you definitely need a uniform to put on. It is not a material uniform but one that will help you to withstand the spiritual attacks of Satan. We will start from the top until we get to the bottom. Let us go to
Ephesians 6:13

"Wherefore take unto you the whole armour of God that ye may be able to withstand in the evil day, and having done all, to stand"

For us to stand against the attacks of the devil we need all of the armour and not just parts of it. This armour is a daily protector that is to be kept on night and day. There is not a time that it has to be taken off. Our armour is Jesus Christ, and He is Jesus Christ the word.

"In the beginning was the Word, and the Word was with God, and the Word was God. The same was in the beginning with God. And the Word was made flesh, and dwelt among us, (and we beheld his glory, the glory as of the only begotten of the Father,)full of grace and truth".

BEES STING

(John 1:1-2 John1;14)

Jesus is our armour and this is an inward armour of protection and not outward bodily protection. Being in the presence of God all the time gives you the armour. Jesus is our Righteousness, our Salvation, and our Truth. This is used to defend the soldier who puts it on. It is used for protection. Along with this is given the Sword of the Spirit. This is a weapon used to attack and drive away Satan. At the same time it helps to scare away the enemy.-In the temptation, Jesus used the Word of God to defeat Satan. Knowing the Word of God enables us to clearly identify the true from the false teachers.

" stand therefore, having your loins girt about with truth Having on the breastplate of righteousness; this is the Righteousness of Christ, which is implanted in us when we receive Christ. This righteousness helps us to reflect the image of Jesus in our daily living. It starts through believing what Jesus did at the cross of Calvary and results in God declaring us to be righteous. It is both, a declaration by God, and an implantation by the Holy Spirit that causes us to live righteously by God's standard. It happens

BEES STING

immediately when we are Born Again and continues to grow as we progress and grow in our commitment.

And your feet shod with the preparation of the gospel of peace; Jesus is the prince of peace, peace can only be found in Jesus Christ. Being shod speaks of having our feet covered in preparation for sharing the Good News with others so they may experience God's love.

Above all, taking the shield of faith, wherewith ye shall be able to quench all the fiery darts of the wicked. Our object of Faith is the finished work of Calvary and all that the work of Christ involves. Our faith is reliable because the one who is the object of our faith is and He never goes back on His promises. **And take the helmet of salvation** our minds being renewed through the knowledge of Christ, "**the sword of the Spirit, which is the word of God**: **knowing that *there are three that bear record in Heaven; the Father, the Word and the Holy Ghost and these three are one Praying always with all prayer and***

BEES STING

supplication in the Spirit, and watching thereunto with all perseverance and supplication for all saints."

(1 John 5:7)

"He gives power to the weak , and to those who have no might He increases strength. Even the youths shall faint and be weary , and the young men shall utterly fall , but those who wait on the Lord shall renew their strength : they shall mount on wings like eagles , they shall run and not be weary , they shall walk and not faint."

(Isaiah 40:29-31)

As you can see from what is previously stated, we are covered from top to bottom in the spiritual realm. Victory can only be experienced when one is well protected. We must remember that the enemy comes to kill, steal and destroy **John 10:10**. Therefore our weapons are not carnal but spiritual to the pulling down of all strongholds.

In the book of **1 Samuel 17;38-39** we are told:

BEES STING

"And Saul armed David with his armour, and he put an helmet of brass upon his head; also he armed him with a coat of mail. And David girded his sword upon his armour, and he assayed to go; for he had not proved it. And David said unto Saul, I cannot go with these; for I have not proved them. And David put them from him".

Saul offered David physical armour when he confronted Goliath. David rejected it because he had not been properly trained and prepared to use it and David knew that goliath could only be killed by a higher power. In **1 Samuel 17:45**

"Then said David to the Philistine, Thou comest to me with a sword, and With a spear, and with a shield: but I come to thee in the name of the LORD of hosts, the God of the armies of Israel, whom thou hast defied. This day will the LORD deliver thee into mine hand; and I will smite thee, and take thine head from thee; and I will give the carcases of the host of the Philistines this day unto the fowls of the air, and to the wild beasts of the earth; that all the earth may know that there is a God in Israel. And all this assembly shall know that the LORD saveth not with sword and

BEES STING

spear: for the battle is the LORD'S, and he will give you into our hands."

David understood then that victory was from God even as we understand it now. David knew that the only way he was going to win was to confront the enemy with the only weapon which he was familiar with and that was faith in God. He knew that God was His only hope; God is the only one who fights our battles and wins them. The enemy comes to us with physical weapons and armour but we defeat him through spiritual armour and weapons.

Remember, all of our armour is spiritual; we access the spiritual realm through prayer and supplication. To achieve victory in any situation, a child of God needs to put on the full armour throughout without fail. The stronger the spiritual walk the stronger the armour. We need to be right with God, walking in humbleness and ready to repent and seeking God's face every moment of every day.

Let us Pray

Yahweh we thank you for you grace and mercy, we thank you for setting us free.

BEES STING

Jehovah God we pray in the name of Jesus that you will help us to depart from evil and do good, seek peace and pursue it. Behold I was shapen in iniquiy and in sin did my mother conceive me. Purge me with thy hyssop and I shall be clean, wash me , and I shall be whiter than snow Create in me a clean heart o God and renew the right spirit within me . Cast me not away from thy presence and take not thy Holy Spirit from me. Amen.

Sword

Romans 13:12" The night is far spent, the day is at hand: let us therefore cast off the works of darkness, and let us put on the armour of light."

2 Corinthians 6:7" By the word of truth, by the power of God, by the armour of righteousness on the right hand and on the left",

Psalm 64;2" Hide me from the secret counsel of the wicked; from the insurrection of the workers of iniquity:"

BEES STING

Psalm 69:15-16" Deliver me out of the mire, and let me not sink: let me be delivered from them that hate me, and out of the deep waters. Let not the water flood overflow me, neither let the deep swallow me up, and let not the pit shut her mouth upon me".

Grandma stretched herself and yawned like a kitten ready to fall asleep. Nhamo remained in deep thought over what he had just heard. He made Jane a cup of tea at her request and brought grandma her water. As he contemplated on what he just heard a picture began to form in his mind as his understanding became clearer. He realized that things were not going to be easy. He knew now that he had eternal life and he didn't have to fear being eternally separated from God.

There are your drinks grandma and Jane. Jane, it will be your turn next to go and make us some tea. Grandma smelled something good coming from the kitchen. I think that lunch will be here soon she said. We will continue

BEES STING

tomorrow and I will answer any other questions that you may have.

We all agreed to grandma's suggestion. Nhamo also wanted an excuse to chat with Jane alone. They had a lot to catch up on since they had last seen and talked seriously to each other. They had a wonderful lunch and decided to walk down to the river and enjoy the scenery. They watched the little tadpoles swimming in the water. Further down the river there was a small boat with two fishermen trying to catch their dinner? How wonderful to enjoy nature and its riches. Jane skipped around singing:

How great is our God.

Singing how great is our God The name

above all names

Worthy to be praised

How great is our God.

When she stopped Nhamo was dumbfounded. He was so intrigued by her sweet voice and asked her to teach him the words and how to sing them It was an afternoon well

BEES STING

spent. He went to bed early looking forward to the following day.

BEES STING

On the run

BEES STING

At 3 a.m. Nhamo was wakened by a strange noise coming from his room. He felt as if his bed was being rocked. He switched on the light and looked under the bed but there was nothing. He switched off the light and went back to bed. The commotion started again and he began to panic. He was really scared. As the rocking intensified, he jumped out of bed, switched on the light, and ran towards his grandma's bedroom. Whatever it was, he was not going to let it get him.

He knocked on his grandma's bedroom and quickly went in. She asked what the matter was. She showed no sign of fear. Now his heart was beating fiercely and he could hardly breathe. For a second he could not speak. He was tongue tied. Nhamo struggled to calm himself down as grandma sat up in her bed and turned on her bedside light. He was sweating in fear, and grandma asked what the matter was.

He told her about the rocking bed. She laughed and then she said what a shame that he has not learned that yet. He asked her what she meant; she told him that she would leave it until

BEES STING

the morning. He asked her what he was supposed to do? She told him to read

2 Timothy 1:7

"For God has not given us the spirit of fear, but of power and of love, and of a sound mind." Think about the meaning of this scripture and pray.

    Nhamo was awakened by his grandma stamping her stick on the floor next to his bed. He opened his eyes to see her standing next to his bed and telling him to get up because he overslept his usual time. He thanked her for waking him and she left his room. He sat up in bed and pushed the covers off.

    He prayed a short prayer and prepared himself for the day. He double checked under his bed to see if there was anything there. Satisfied that there was nothing, he left the room.

    Nhamo was surprised to see Jane already seated next to his grandma. They were enjoying a lovely breakfast and each others company.

BEES STING

He walked in and greeted both and sat himself on the other side of the table grandma.

BEES STING

Agag must die

BEES STING

Grandma turned to me and reviewed the previous night's activities. Nhamo was a bit embarrassed in front of Jane but worth hearing what grandma had to say. Grandma spoke about having courage to stand without being afraid.

She asked us to open **2 Timothy 1; 7**

"For God hath not given us the spirit of fear; but of power, and of love, and of a sound mind"

Fear does not come from God but comes from not trusting God. The devil causes fear by causing us to focus on our circumstances. Fear is the opposite of trusting in God. So Nhamo, when you came running into my room last night Faith was out and fear was in. That moment was a time that you doubted God's protection. The fear was caused by forces opposed to faith causing you to question God's presence and protection. "**Without faith we cannot please God. Hebrews" 11:6**

Ephesians 6:16 tells us that " Above all, taking the shield of faith, wherewith ye shall be able to quench all the fiery darts of

BEES STING

the wicked." Faith is our invisible shield that protects us from the fiery darts of the enemy. So when you find yourself in any situation use your Faith as your defence mechanism. I will teach you more about faith another day but for now I just wanted to explain what you should have done yesterday before you came to me. I will explain what you should have done yesterday instead of running to me. ***In Psalm 56:3*** *here is a verse to remember when we are afraid*

"What times I am afraid, I will trust in thee."

Today I want to share with you a story from the book of ***1Samuel 15:9***
"But Saul and the people spared Agag, and the best of the sheep, and of the oxen, and of the fatlings, and the lambs, and all that was good, and would not utterly destroy them: but everything that was vile and refuse, that they destroyed utterly.

Agag was the king of the Amalakites some 500 years before, when Israel was in the wilderness. Having just come out of Egypt, the people of God were attacked by the Amalakites.

BEES STING

"Then came Amalek, and fought with Israel in Rephidm. And Moses said unto Joshua, Choose us out men, and go out, fight with Amalek: to morrow I will stand on the top of the hill with the rod of God in mine hand.

So Joshua did as Moses had said to him, and fought with Amalek: and Moses, Aaron, and Hur went up to the top of the hill. And it came to pass, when Moses held up his hand, that Israel prevailed: and when he let down his hand, Amalek prevailed.

But Moses' hands were heavy; and they took a stone, and put it under him, and he sat thereon; and Aaron and Hur stayed up his hands, the one on the one side, and the other on the other side; and his hands were steady until the going down of the sun.

And Joshua discomfited Amalek and his people with the edge of the sword. And the LORD said unto Moses, Write this for a memorial in a book, and rehearse it in the ears of Joshua: for I will utterly put out the remembrance of Amalek from under heaven. And Moses built an altar, and called the name of it Jehovah Nissi: For he

BEES STING

said, Because the LORD hath sworn that the LORD will have war with Amalek from generation to generation.
(Exodus 17: 8-16: 8)

Saul was supposed to destroy Agog the king and all that belonged to him including people and all that they owned. But Saul decided to spare Agag and the best of his sheep, oxen, lambs and anything that looked good . This was in opposition to what God had commanded.

" Now go and smite Amalek, and utterly destroy all that they have, and spare them not; but slay both man and woman, infant and suckling, ox and sheep, camel and ass."
(I Samuel 15;3)

Everything was to be destroyed but Saul did not obey God. Agag represents our fleshly desires. When you become a Christian all fleshly things that is things that are against the word of God must be crucified. (That means we should count ourselves as dead to them, no longer having interest in feeding them.) There are things in our lives of which we need to let go, once we are born again. If we do not "let go," those same things will wind up hurting us and

BEES STING

become like thorns in our heel and hinder our walk with Christ.

That is exactly what happened to the children of Israel when they spared King Agog. In spite of the Prophet Samuel's confronting Saul over the matter, Saul tried to justify himself as to why he spared Agag and his treasures.

"***And Saul said unto Samuel, Yea, I have obeyed the voice of the LORD, and have gone the way which the LORD sent me, and have brought Agag the king of Amalek, and have utterly destroyed the Amalekites. But the people took of the spoil, sheep and oxen, the chief of the things which should have been utterly destroyed, to sacrifice unto the LORD thy God in Gilgal".***
(1 Samuel 15:20)

For that reason Saul was rejected by God.
"And Samuel said, Hath the LORD as great delight in burnt offerings and sacrifices, as in obeying the voice of the LORD? Behold, to obey is better than sacrifice, and to hearken than the fat of rams. For rebellion is as the sin of witchcraft, and stubbornness is as iniquity and idolatry.

BEES STING

Because thou hast rejected the word of the LORD, he hath also rejected thee from being king"
(1Samuel 15:23)

Jane and Nhamo are you listening to what I am saying? Yes grandma, they quickly answered in unison. Grandma continued and said that is why I am telling you today that your Agag must die. Any fleshly pleasure that you are clinging to must be removed out of your life. There are some who are living in adultery, fornication, gossiping, lying and worshipping ancestral spirits. They go to the witch doctors at night and sing in the Praise and worship team Sunday morning. Some fly on broom sticks at night and go under the sea to perform their rituals and have high profile positions in the church. Some are driven by self ambitions and selfish motives. You can not sacrifice that which God has rejected. God is looking for a pure sacrifice from us.

" Now the things of the flesh are manifest which are these Adultery, fornication, uncleanness"

BEES STING

(Galatians 5:19)-

Grandma said all these are that which should be removed far from our lives. Some place their faith on wrong objects like themselves and sometimes even faith in their faith. Some believe they can do things without the help of God and are putting their faith in their ability. This is true of Christians as well as those who are not. There are believers who believe that if they want anything from God they will fast and get it. Then you hear them saying I fasted to get this job, I prayed six times a day, I repeated Psalm 27 for ten days. These are giving glory to themselves. There is nothing wrong with fasting. It is entirely scriptural and necessary at times. The reason for one's fast should be to Glorify God and not to twist God's arm in getting whatever one wants.

"***How art thy fallen from Heaven Lucifer, son of the morning how art thou cast down to the ground, which didst weaken the nations. For thou hast said in thine heart, I will ascend into heaven, I will***

BEES STING

exalt my throne above the stars of God. I will sit also upon the mount of the congregation, in the sides of the north: I will ascend above the heights of the clouds; I will be like the most High".

(Isaiah 14:12-14)

These are the five I's that caused the fall of Satan. Some of us are guilty of doing the same by placing the emphasis on "me". Pride and self-will keep God from hearing our prayers and working in our life.

"If I regard iniquiy in my heart, the Lord will not hear me."

(Psalm 66:18)

That means that if I enjoy having sin around as a permanent guest, it will keep God from blessing me and answering my prayers. It is just like not destroying Agag.

Some have made something other than Jesus and His completed work at calvary as the objects of their faith. Sometimes that which we hold tightly to can cause us to sin against God.

BEES STING

At these words, Nhamo quickly sat up and asked grandma, do you mean that if I hold on to the things of the past that I open the door for the enemy to attack me? Grandma replied that is right and when you open the door the enemy comes like a flood.

Let us Pray

Yahweh we thank you for you grace and mercy. We thank you for setting us free. Jehovah God we pray in the name of Jesus that You will help us to depart from evil and do good, seek peace and pursue it. Behold I was shapen in iniquiy and in sin did my mother conceive me. Purge me with thy hyssop and I shall be clean, wash me , and I shall be whiter than snow Create in me a clean heart o God and renew the right spirit within me . Cast me not away from thy presence and take not thy Holy Spirit from me. Amen.

Sword

Psalm 64:2-6

BEES STING

"Hide me from the secret counsel of the wicked; from the insurrection of the workers of iniquity: Who whet their tongue like a sword, *and* bend *their bows to shoot* their arrows, *even* bitter words: That they may shoot in secret at the perfect: suddenly do they shoot at him, and fear not. They encourage themselves *in* an evil matter: they commune of laying snares privily; they say, who shall see them? They search out iniquities; they accomplish a diligent search: both the inward *thought* of every one *of them*, and the heart, *is* deep.

Luke 9 :23-25 And he said to *them* all, If any *man* will come after me, let him deny himself, and take up his cross daily, and follow me. 24 For whosoever will save his life shall lose it: but whosoever will lose his life for my sake, the same shall save it. For what is a man advantaged, if he gain the whole world, and lose himself, or be cast away?

BEES STING

BEES STING

Afflictions of the righteous are many but God will see you through

BEES STING

In the morning grandma arose at her usual time and prepared herself to face the day. She went outside to begin her usual morning walk. Nhamo visualized her in his mind, taking the route she routinely took every day. She would stop under the Baobab tree, and take in the lovely landscape. She would talk to herself, and pick up some dry leaves, crushing them in her hand and letting the wind gently blow them away. Then she would continue on her journey.

Nhamo was beginning to understand what grandma had been talking about all these days. It was interesting, but grandma had not yet answered Jane's question as to why a Christian continues to suffer. He intended to remind her so she can give them the answers that they wanted to hear. Nhamo readied himself for what was next. He cleaned up, tidied his room, and departed to the dining room where the smell of fried bacon stimulated his appetite. He looked outside through a wide opened window, viewing the sky as blue and clear as far as the eyes could see. No one was in the dining area yet, but he could hear grandma moving about in her bedroom, dropping objects about and singing in

BEES STING

a hoarse rusty voice. He thought to himself, "bless her soul".

She opened her door and called for Nhamo to help her. She invited him into her room and asked him to reach up on top of her cupboard and bring down a diary which appeared to have been there for a long time. The dust from the book caused him to cough as he retrieved it. Grandma chuckled as she held out her hand to receive it.

They made their way to the dining area where they prepared to eat. They sat down to a tasty breakfast and engaged in casual conversation. After breakfast Nhamo cleared the table and thanked the maid for a lovely breakfast, departing outside for a breath of fresh air.

As he walked, he reflected on the message that grandma had been teaching them. They were starting to make sense to him now. He was beginning to understand about his Heavenly Father. Jesus paid all debts of sin through His death. He wondered how he could repay all that Jesus had done for him.

BEES STING

It is not easy to follow Jesus. One cannot do it by their own ability. The more one tries to be independent of God the easier it becomes to stray farther and farther and engage in behaviour that is contrary to the word of God. It is only when we surrender entirely to the Lord, believe what Jesus did at Calvary, and trust fully in His word that the Holy Spirit can direct us.

Suddenly from behind a bush Nhamo could see a beautiful rabbit basking in the sun eating fresh leaves from a nearby bush. He stood captivated by the activity. As he watched this rabbit enjoying himself, he started to imagine what was going through its mind. He imagined the rabbit being grateful to have a meal (rather than being one for a dog). From his left he heard gentle rustling grass and as he turned, he saw his grandma's dog lying flat on its stomach, ready to strike the rabbit.

Before he could warn the rabbit, the dog leapt into the air and pounced on it, making it his next meal. The rabbit had no chance. The dog was happy that he had a meal but the rabbit was gone.

BEES STING

This is how life is; one time you are on top of the mountain happy and enjoying yourself, and the next instant it is all finished. This event touched his heart and as he headed back he started to think about what he had just witnessed.

As he walked closer to the house he saw Jane. He called to her and she stopped and waited for him. Nhamo caught up with her and they started walking together, laughing and sharing their different experiences.

They entered the house and found grandma talking to her maid. They were laughing and looked more like sisters than employer and employee. She turned around and seeing us called us to come in and join the merry party.

They went in and sat down; Jane sat next to grandma and told her that the following day she was leaving for the town. Grandma said that she was going to miss her. Jane assured her that she would be back before we even noticed that she was gone

BEES STING

Grandma adjusted her cushions and looked at us thoughtfully. She turned to Jane and said, Now Jane, it is time to answer your question as to why you are suffering so much after you have received Christ. Turn to

Psalm 34:17-20

"When the righteous cry for help, the Lord hears and delivers them out of all their troubles. The Lord is near to the broken hearted and saves the crushed in spirit. Many are the afflictions of the righteous, but the Lord delivers him out of them all. He keeps all his bones; not one of them is broken."

This Scripture tells us that there are going to be problems but God hears the cry of His children and delivers them. Although there will be many afflictions, we shall not be confounded by them. When you receive Christ, you have enlisted in the army of God. The adversary, the devil, comes after you with the purpose to kill, steal, and destroy anything that will bring us closer to God. The adversary will touch your health, your finances, your marriage and your spiritual life.

BEES STING

The aim of the adversary is to discourage you and to make you doubt the word of God. Our God is a good God.

"No temptation has overtaken you that is not common to man. God is faithful, and he will not let you be tempted beyond your ability, but with the temptation he will also provide the way of escape, that you may be able to endure it."

(1 Corinthians 10:13)

Even in your problems, troubles and afflictions, God is there and He Has already provided a solution. Paul in the book of Romans Said:

"For I consider that the sufferings of this present time are not worth comparing with the glory that is to be revealed to us."

(Romans 8:18)

All the encounters we go through on this earth are not worthy of loss of sleep. Because they are temporary they will not last for ever. There is a greater reward awaiting the Christian.

BEES STING

In Glory, but for now, trials are necessary to remove impurities from our life.

In **Romans 5:3-4** Paul *said:*

*" **More than that, we rejoice in our sufferings, knowing that suffering produces endurance, and endurance produces character, and character produces hope."***

Our suffering is not because of what we have done but what we must go through in order to produce character. We are no longer condemned. Jesus settled that matter at Calvary.

***"There is therefore now no more condemnation to them which are in Christ Jesus, who walk not after the flesh, but after the Spirit.* "**

(Romans 8:1)

You two must find time to read the book of Job. Job was a righteous man who was righteous in the eyes of God but he had to go through tribulation but he never stopped believing God.

"We are troubled, on every side yet not distressed, we are perplexed, but not in

BEES STING

despair; Persecuted, but not forsaken, cast down but not destroyed."

(2 Corinthians 4:8 – 9)

The life of a Christian is not easy and smooth but in all that we go through, we know that Yahweh our God is in control and we will never be confounded by tribulation.

Yahweh we thank you as we come before your throne today. Yahweh We acknowledges your Lordship in our lives. You are our refuge, our fortress, our hiding place. Your hand is not short that you cannot save us; neither your ear too heavy that you cannot hear us.

No weapon that is formed against shall prosper, and every tongue that shall rise against us in judgement thou shalt condemn.

We are more than conquerors through Jesus Christ. We are the head and not the tail, we are above and not beneath.

The Lord is our portion, saith my soul: therefore will I hope in him. The Lord is

BEES STING

good unto them that wait for Him, to the soul that seeketh Him. Amen.

Amen and Amen Nhamo repeated to himself. Remembering the bees that stung him, he recalled that although it was so painful, the moment he drew out the honey from the honeycomb and started to eat it all the pain vanished from his body. It is the same for the Christian. All the trials that a child of God suffers is just for a short time.

There is honey waiting for us when we stop trusting in this earthly vessel and begin to live in our heavenly bodies. There will be no more sorrow, no more pain; no more tears but there will be joy, everlasting joy, which will never be compared to this earthly suffering. Peter encourages us in our trials by these words; "**Beloved, think it not strange concerning the fiery trials that shall try you, as though some strange thing happened unto you, but rejoice inasmuch as ye a re partakers of Christ's sufferings that when His glory shall be revealed, ye may be glad also with exceeding joy. "**

BEES STING

(I Peter 4:12)

Heaven will be sweeter than honey can ever be. Its sweetness surpasses any form of pain. Beyond the pain there is blessing that awaits us. Behind the pain of child birth there is a lovely baby; beyond the pain of studying there is joy of passing, beyond hard work there is joy in harvesting.

BEES STING

Printed in Great Britain
by Amazon.co.uk, Ltd.,
Marston Gate.